Written by Mary D. Wade • Illustrated by Virginia Roeder

Cover design by Gray Communications

Printed in the United States of America by Color Art, Inc., St. Louis

10 9 8 7 6 5 4 3 2 1

My Little chickadee

The Massachusetts state bird is the chickadee.
It likes to hang upside down as it eats at a feeder.

Use a yellow crayon to color the shapes that have a dot.
Use a black crayon to color the shapes that have a star.

STATE FLOWER

The state flower is the mayflower. Sometimes this plant is called trailing arbutus or ground laurel. The pink or white flowers have five petals.

Can you find the vine that connects to the flowers? Then color the flowers. Start with the vine in the lower right-hand corner.

a fishy Puzzle

The cod is the state fish. In honor of the importance of fishing, Massachusetts hung a five-foot-long wooden codfish in the House of Representatives in Boston two hundred years ago. As a prank, someone once stole the cod, but the police got it back.

Can you find the cod?

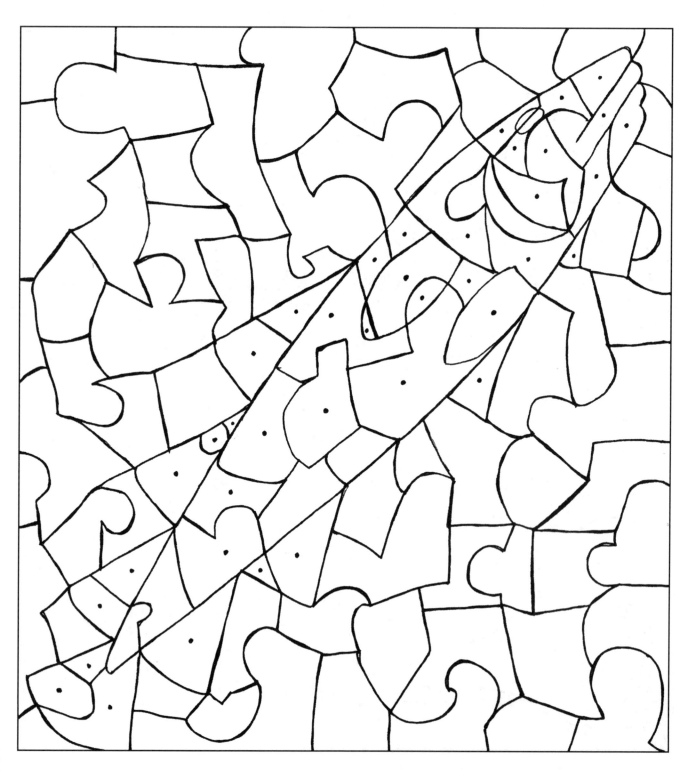

SHADE IN SUMMER

The American elm is the Massachusetts state tree. The trees in Massachusetts turn beautiful colors in the fall.

Color the elm tree according to the numbers.

1 = Green   2 = Yellow   3 = Orange

A Lovely Predator

A second-grade class suggested the ladybug as the Massachusetts state insect.

Use a black crayon to color the shapes with the number 1.
Use a red crayon to color the shapes with the number 2.
Use a green crayon to color the shapes with the number 3.

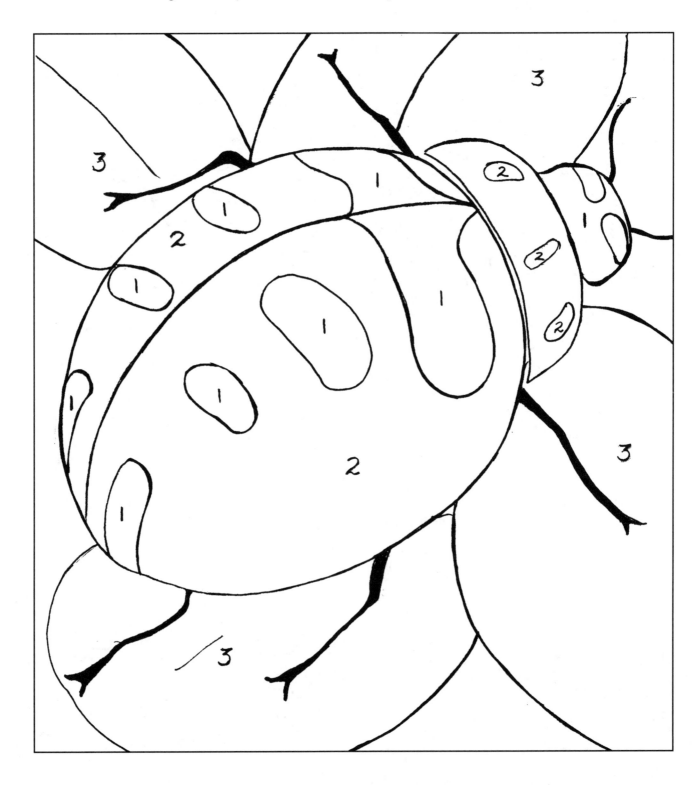

RHODONITE

The Massachusetts state gem is rhodonite. It varies in color from light pink to deep rose. Massachusetts is known for making college and high school class rings.

Can you find the five rings hidden in this carnival picture? Each has a setting of rhodonite. Color each ring gold. Then color the gemstone any shade of pink you like.

Fruit from a Marsh

The Massachusetts state beverage is cranberry juice.

Can you match the juice glasses?

DENIZEN OF THE DEEP

The state marine animal is the right whale.
Sailors called it "right" because it was easy to capture and get the oil.

Can you find the whale?

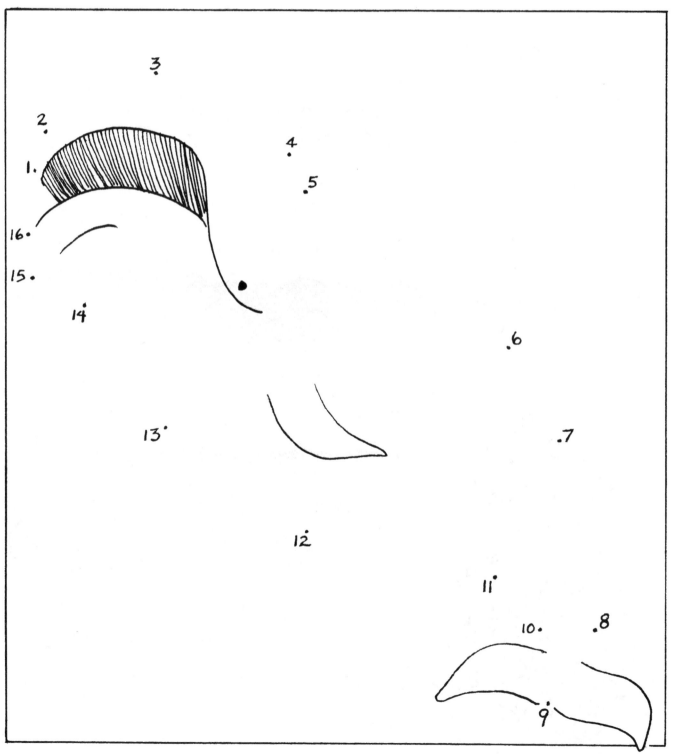

A CORNY SNACK

The state muffin is the corn muffin. On this ear of corn,
color all the kernels that have a dot. What is the message?

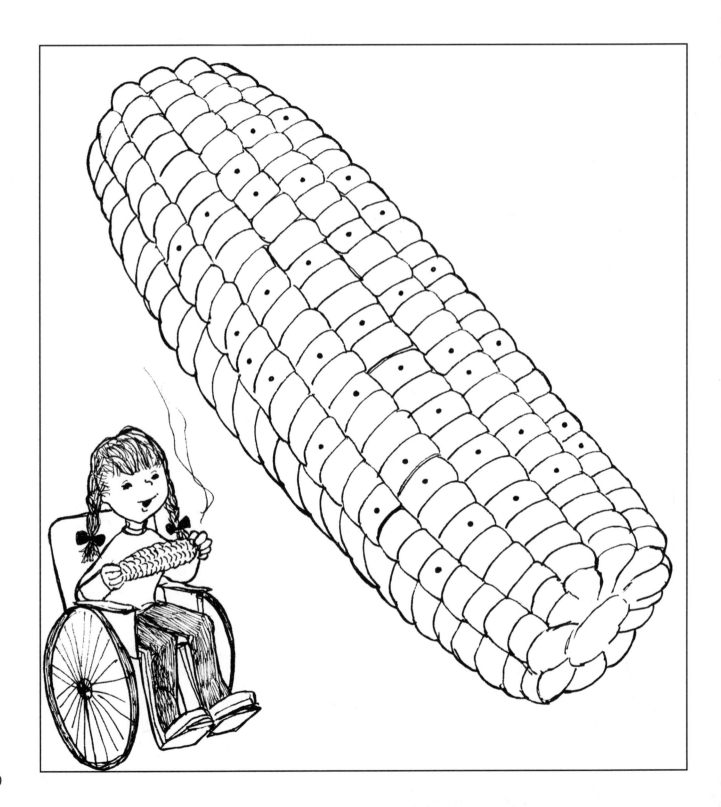

Wonderful Pups

The Boston terrier is the state dog. The first one was bred in Boston in 1870. Can you match these Boston terriers?

A Jolly Carnivore

The state dinosaur is the theropod. Actually, the theropods are a group of dinosaurs. Almost all predatory dinosaurs are theropods.

Follow this theropod's tracks with a red crayon. Can you read the message?

ROLL THAT ROCK

Plymouth Rock is the state rock. The Pilgrims landed in 1620, but they didn't carve the date on the rock. Nobody can prove that the Pilgrims even stepped out on this rock. It was moved around town but is finally back at the ocean.

Can you get it from the water back to the center of town?

A New Home

There were 102 Pilgrims who came to America from England.

Use the letter key to solve the puzzle and find something they used.

Key:

W	A	P	E	M	L	R	Y	K	F	O
1	2	3	4	5	6	7	8	9	10	11

___ ___ ___ ___ ___ ___ ___ ___
 5   2   8   10   6   11   1   7

GrAtItUDE

The first Thanksgiving was celebrated in Plymouth, Massachusetts, in 1621.
Can you fill in the blanks in the story below? Use the words under the picture.

USED   ONLY   LONG   HARVEST
MANY   THEY   YOUNG   PILGRIMS

P _ _ _ _ _ S CAME TO AMERICA.

IT WAS A L _ _ G, HARD VOYAGE.

Y _ _ _ G CHILDREN CAME, TOO.

M _ _ Y PEOPLE DIED THAT FIRST YEAR.

O _ _ Y SQUANTO KNEW HOW TO GROW CORN.

THEY U _ _ D NETS TO CATCH FISH.

T _ _ Y PUT FISH AND CORN IN THE GROUND.

A GOOD H _ _ _ _ _ T MADE THEM THANKFUL.

WHAT'S IN A NAME?

Some Pilgrim children had names that seem strange to us today.
Other Pilgrim first names are familiar. Look across and down
to find the names of these Pilgrim children.

Love   Peregrine   Mary
Wrestling   John   Elizabeth
Remember   Samuel   Ellen
Resolved   Joseph   Richard

S A M U E L E I S
J U D Y R X L P U
J O H N N V I E Z
K F I J I Q Z R I
S T R O E N A E E
I R A S Z O B G T
R E M E M B E R H
I S C P A T T I A
C O T H R W H N N
H L O N Y D O E K
A V E O B I L L F
R E R N S T A L U
D D Q M L O V E L
W R E S T L I N G

Potluck

Chief Massasoit brought ninety of his fellow Wampanoag Indians to celebrate Thanksgiving with the Pilgrims. He knew that there would not be enough food. His men went into the forest to get more.

Can you substitute the next letter in the alphabet for the letter that is printed? That will tell you what the hunters brought back.

$\overline{C}$ $\overline{D}$ $\overline{D}$ $\overline{Q}$ $\overline{S}$ $\overline{T}$ $\overline{Q}$ $\overline{J}$ $\overline{D}$ $\overline{X}$

Let's Eat

Can you find these foods that were served at the first Thanksgiving? Look across and down.

turkey	squash	corn	fish
deer	pumpkin	cranberries	

C O O K I E S O P M Z
A C H I C K E N U I Q
F I S H L G M T M L E
I T Q U A I C J P K G
G U U T I D O L K N G
C R A N B E R R I E S
D K S L U E N H N U T
R E H N G R A P E S A
I Y A M S S O D A Z E

Cranberry Fun

Some people make decorations by threading cranberries and popcorn on a string. Can you trace the popcorn string to spell out a message?

Scrimshaw

When sailors got bored on long voyages, they carved whale bones and teeth. They made pictures of ships and animals by scratching tiny lines. This is called scrimshaw. Artists use other materials today for scrimshaw carving because whales are endangered.

Make your own scrimshaw picture by drawing tiny black lines.
It could be your house, your pet, or whatever you like.

THE LIGHT GLEAMS
AND IS GONE

Lighthouses along the Atlantic Ocean shore warn ships about dangerous rocks. This picture got scrambled. Can you put it back together correctly?

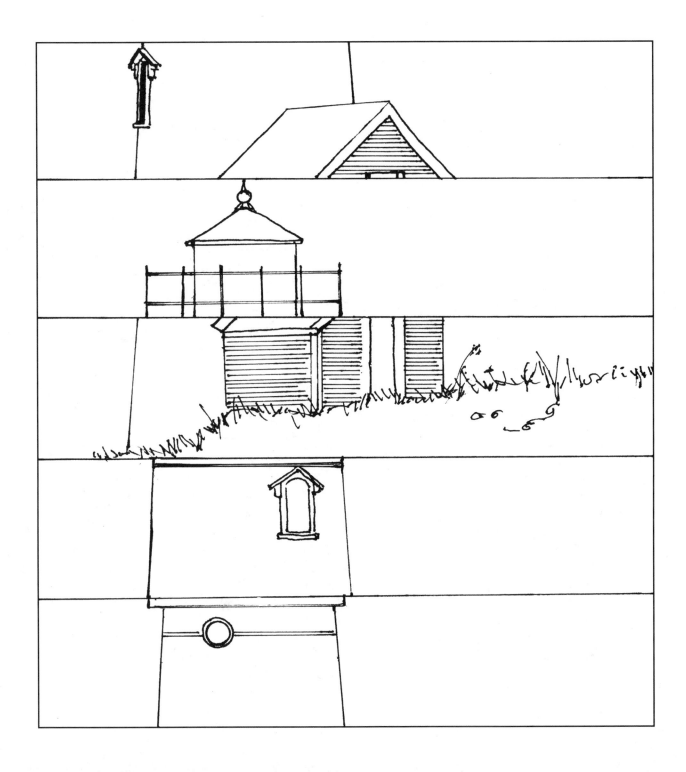

DEEP AND DARK BLUE OCEAN

The Cape Cod National Seashore stretches along the eastern edge of the cape. Atlantic Ocean water is cold, but people on the beach enjoy the cool breeze.

Can you find six starfish in this picture?

What a Catch!

Fishing is still an important industry in Massachusetts. Look across and down to find these marine animal names in the puzzle.

cod   crab   shrimp   haddock   tuna   herring

lobster   clam   flounder   scallop   swordfish

```
L  E  S  C  A  L  L  O  P
L  J  I  H  E  L  A  D  O
O  A  F  E  H  C  L  A  M
B  M  L  R  A  B  E  E  F
S  W  O  R  D  F  I  S  H
T  H  U  I  D  I  C  O  D
E  E  N  O  A  T  S  T
R  A  D  G  C  R  A  B  U
W  T  E  X  K  A  L  F  N
S  H  R  I  M  P  Z  E  A
```

ON THE SLOPES

Because the winters are cold in Massachusetts, skiers have fun on the snow.
In this picture there are eight things wrong. Can you find them?

UP TO THE MINUTE

At the beginning of the American Revolution, Minutemen were at Lexington and Concord.
They got their name because they said they could be ready to fight in 60 seconds.
Six letters are scattered all over this picture. Can you unscramble them?
You will learn the occupation of most Minutemen.

BREED'S HILL

The Battle of Bunker Hill was one of the first big battles of the American Revolution. It actually took place on Breed's Hill. That is where the monument is.

Connect the dots to see what the monument looks like.

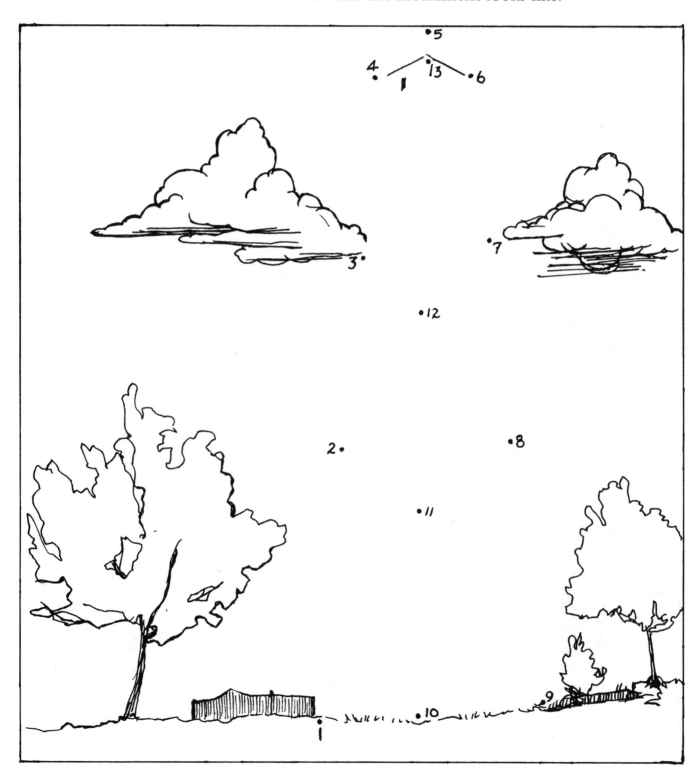

PLAIN AS DAY

Massachusetts lawmaker John Hancock signed his name first on the Declaration of Independence. He wrote very large because he said he wanted King George III to read it without his glasses.

Write your name the same way he wrote his.
Then make up four other fancy ways to write your name.

To Arms

Deborah Sampson was an indentured servant. Indentured servants were like temporary slaves. When her time of service was up, she made herself a man's suit. She wore the suit when she joined George Washington's army. She said her name was Robert Shurtleff. After the war, the government gave her a pension.

Look at her two names. Cross off the letters that are found in both names.

DEBORAH SAMPSON
ROBERT SHURTLEFF

Write each different letter that is left on Deborah's real name.

___ ___ ___ ___ ___

Use these letters to make as many words as you can.
You should get at least six. One is a name.

_____ _____ _____

_____ _____ _____

_____ _____ _____

_____ _____ _____

METALSMITH

Paul Revere was famous for his ride to warn the colonists that British soldiers were coming. However, he was just as famous for making things out of metal.

Find out which metals he used by matching the number with a letter.
Then draw a line to the thing made of that metal.

Key: L I N C V R S O G E P D
      1 2 3 4 5 6 7 8 9 10 11 12

‾ ‾ ‾ ‾ ‾ ‾
7 2 1 5 10 6

‾ ‾ ‾ ‾
2 6 8 3

‾ ‾ ‾ ‾ ‾ ‾
4 8 11 11 10 6

Famous as Can Be

Some people think a very important woman is buried in an old cemetery in the middle of Boston. Everyone knows her name. Find out what it is by filling in the missing letters in these nursery rhymes.

HICKORY DICKORY DOCK
THE __OUSE RAN UP THE CL__CK
THE CLOCK S__RUCK ONE.
T_E MOUS__ RAN DOWN.
HICKO__Y DICKORY DOCK.

MARY, MARY, QUITE CONTRARY,
HOW DOES YOUR __ARDEN GR__W?
WITH SILVER BELLS, AND C__CKLE__HELLS,
AND PR__TTY MAIDS ALL IN A ROW.

Everyone called her __ __ __ __ __ __ __   __ __ __ __ __ .

Way Up There

The highest point in the state is Mount Greylock. It is 3,491 feet above sea level.
On a clear day, a person standing on top of Mount Greylock can see these other states.

Can you unscramble their names?

EWN KORY

_____

VOTRMEN

_____

WEN SHERMAHIP

_____

The Rivers Shall Flow

Several rivers run through Massachusetts.
Can you find their names? Look across and down.

Connecticut	Charles	Deerfield
Housatonic	Merrimack	Concord

```
M  E  R  R  I  M  A  C  K  S  O
X  H  O  U  S  A  T  O  N  I  C
R  H  I  N  D  A  N  U  B  E  L
U  V  O  L  E  L  B  E  H  R  O
C  O  N  N  E  C  T  I  C  U  T
H  L  I  B  R  X  Z  Q  O  D  A
A  G  L  A  F  T  O  N  N  U  I
R  A  E  T  I  V  E  X  C  W  T
L  O  E  S  E  I  N  E  O  F  Y
E  A  S  T  L  U  D  Q  R  G  I
S  S  H  U  D  S  O  N  D  L  A
```

FOREST DWELLERS

More than half of Massachusetts is forest land.
These animals are hiding in the forest. Can you find them?

deer   rabbit   skunk   porcupine
snake   owl   raccoon

SWEET MAPLE

Sugaring time comes in early spring. Trees are tapped, and buckets catch the sap. The sap is boiled to make maple syrup.

Can you find the tree that does not have a bucket to catch the sap?

QUITE A MOUTHFUL

Chaugoggagogmanchaugagoggchaubunagungamaugg has the longest name of any place in the world. The name of this lake means "You fish on your side, I fish on my side, and nobody fishes in the middle." Most people use its other name.

Fish out the letters and spell the lake's shorter name. It starts with a W.

Densely Populated Areas

Find the names of these Massachusetts cities and towns: Boston, Amherst, New Bedford, Provincetown, Worcester, Stockbridge, Cambridge, Brookline, Springfield, Fall River, Plymouth, and Lowell. Look across and down.

```
P  R  I  W  O  R  C  E  S  T  E  R
E  C  A  M  B  R  I  D  G  E  T  O
R  S  T  O  C  K  B  R  I  D  G  E
T  T  X  R  S  A  L  T  O  N  Z  T
H  A  H  B  P  A  R  I  S  B  N  N
X  R  B  B  R  O  M  E  G  Y  E  E
P  R  O  V  I  N  C  E  T  O  W  N
L  T  S  S  N  O  A  D  O  S  B  B
Y  O  T  A  G  M  I  E  L  L  E  R
M  N  O  N  F  E  R  L  E  O  D  O
O  X  N  O  I  J  O  H  D  N  F  O
U  L  O  W  E  L  L  I  O  A  O  K
T  F  A  L  L  R  I  V  E  R  R  L
H  X  F  Z  D  B  O  R  N  E  D  I
X  A  M  H  E  R  S  T  O  W  N  N
T  L  A  T  E  L  O  L  C  O  V  E
```

Home of the Bean and the Cod

Solve this anagram of the name of a city in Massachusetts.

___ A K E D   B E A N S   (Yum, yum)

___ L D   N O R T H   C H U R C H   (Ride, Paul Revere, ride)

___ T A T E   C A P I T O L   (Home of the sacred cod)

___ E A   P A R T Y   (Dump it out)

___ L D   S O U T H   M E E T I N G   H O U S E   (Where rebels gather)

___ E W   E N G L A N D   A Q U A R I U M   (Pretty fishy)

Under the Stars

The Boston Pops Orchestra plays an outdoor concert each Fourth of July. When the music gets to a certain place in the *1812 Overture*, howitzer guns are fired.

Something is wrong with this orchestra. Can you find eight things that are not right?

SHIN SPLINTS

The Boston Marathon is the oldest marathon in the United States.

Can you find nine things wrong in this race?

THE SLUGGERS

Fenway Park has been the home of the Boston Red Sox since 1912. Over the years, players smashed many balls into the big fence at the edge of the field.

Follow the smudges on the Green Monster and find the name of one of the Red Sox's greatest players.

CLIDING ON THE LAGOON

Swan boats are fun to ride. They drift serenely
on the lagoon in the Public Garden near Boston Common.

Can you find the missing part of the swan boat?

Jolly Good Books

Massachusetts had the first public library in the United States. Books by favorite Massachusetts authors are on the shelves of the Boston Public Library, but there seems to be a problem.

Can you straighten out these titles?

HAT IN THE CAT   _____

WAY DUCKLINGS MAKE FOR   _____

EGGS AND GREEN HAM   _____

MOON GOODNIGHT   _____

GOOSE TALES MOTHER   _____

ON HOP POP   _____

HIS MULLIGAN STEAM
    SHOVEL AND MIKE   _____

My Country 'tis of Thee

Francis Bellamy wrote something that everybody in the United States should know. It was first published on September 8, 1892, in a Boston publication called *Youth's Companion*. It is printed below, but the letters A and E are missing.

Fill them in so that you can read it.

```
I  PL_DG_  _LLEGI_NC_  TO  TH_

FL_G  OF  TH_  UNIT_D  ST_T_S  OF

_M_RIC_,  _ND  TO  TH_

R_PUBLIC  FOR  WHICH  IT  ST_NDS,

ON_  N_TION  UND_R  GOD,

INDIVISIBL_, WITH  LIB_RTY  _ND

JUSTIC_  FOR  _LL.
```

Tip-off

The Boston Celtics played basketball at the old Boston Garden.
The building was torn down, and the Fleet Center replaced it.
Pieces of the wooden floor were sold or given away.

Look at the pieces around the edge of the picture.
Which one will go in the missing part of the floor?

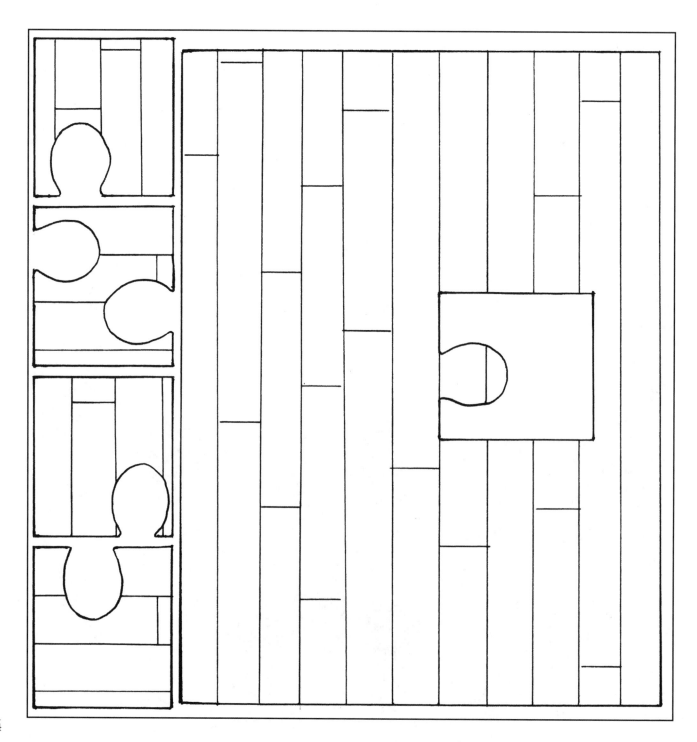

GOAL TO GO

The Boston Bruins play at the Fleet Center. The Boston ice hockey player in the lower left-hand corner of the picture has just made a shot.

Mark the path that takes the puck to the goal.

Neither Snow, nor Rain

Massachusetts had the first post office in America. Help the
letter carrier deliver the letters to the right houses.

A MEDICAL DISCOVERY

A painkiller called ether was first used during an operation at Massachusetts General Hospital in 1846. William Morton of Charlestown was the first person to use this compound on his patients.

What was his occupation? In the blank, place the alphabet letter that comes BEFORE the printed letter.

___ ___ ___ ___ ___ ___ ___
E   F   O   U   J   T   U

A Factory Town

In 1826, Lowell became the first big manufacturing city in the United States.
The Lowell mills made cloth. This piece of cloth has a special picture woven into it.

Color the areas with the number 1 red.
Color the areas with the number 2 blue.

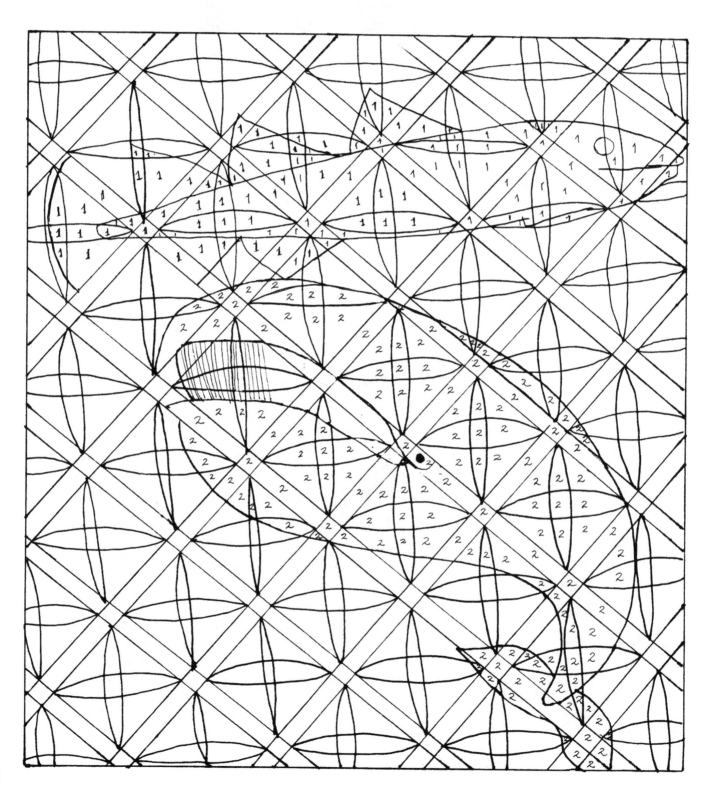

If the Shoe Fits

Massachusetts led the nation in shoe manufacturing in the 1860s.

A customer has tried on many pairs of shoes in this store.
Put the shoes back in the correct boxes.

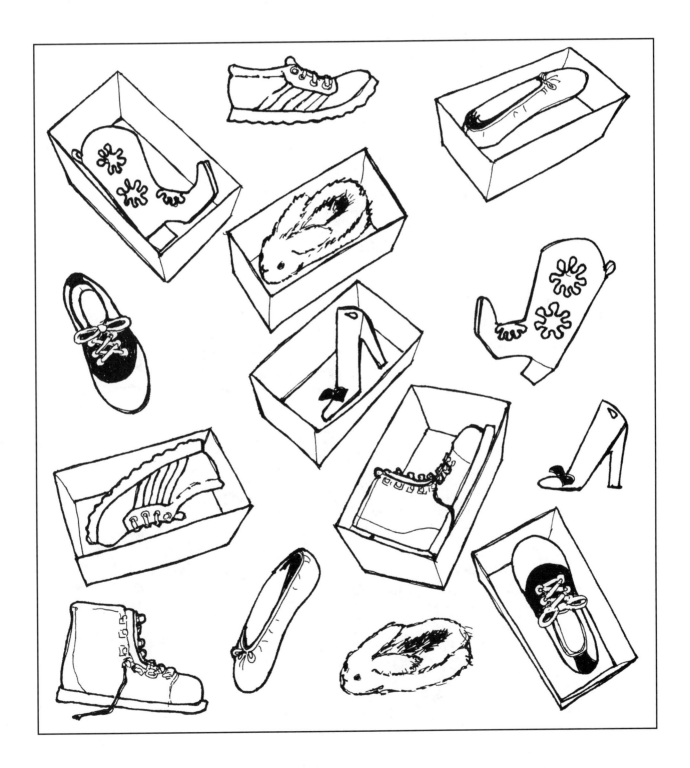

Out for a Spin

When cars were first being built, the Stanley twins were Massachusetts' most successful automobile manufacturer. Their car was the Stanley Steamer.

Find out the twins' first names by substituting letters for the numbers.

Key:

N	I	R	E	C	F	A	L	S
1	2	3	4	5	6	7	8	9

__ __ __ __ __ __ __
6   3   7   1   5   2   9

and

__ __ __ __ __ __ __
6   3   4   4   8   7   1

HECTIC RUSH HOUR

A "Zipper" truck moves a long line of concrete barriers on the roadway twice a day. The truck looks like a zipper when it picks up each barrier and moves it to the other side of a special lane. Cars use the lane to go one way in the morning and another in the afternoon.

Find eight things wrong in this picture.

Hearts and Flowers

Esther Howland lived in Worcester. She created beautiful valentines
and helped make Valentine's Day a popular holiday.

Color and decorate the valentine. Create your own message to put in the center.

MORSE CODE

Samuel Finley Breese Morse was born in Boston. He was a good portrait painter, but he is better known for inventing the telegraph. His invention used a series of dots and dashes to send messages long distances.

Follow the telegraph line. Write each letter as you come to it. What is the message?

DISASTER RELIEF

Clara Barton was born in Oxford. She got the nickname "Angel of the Battlefield" because she nursed soldiers during the Civil War. She also started a famous organization that helps people when their houses are destroyed by floods, earthquakes, or other disasters.

Color the dotted shapes with a red crayon,
and you will learn the name of this organization.

The Vote

Susan B. Anthony and Lucy Stone worked for a law that gave women the right to vote. That happened when the Nineteenth Amendment to the U.S. Constitution was passed. Lucy was born in West Brookfield in 1818. Susan was born in Adams in 1820.

Can you help Susan roll her hoop to Lucy?

Abolishing Slavery

William Lloyd Garrison believed slavery was wrong. He started a newspaper in 1831 that tried to stop slavery. Fill in the name of the newspaper by substituting letters for the numbers.

Key:
B	L	A	O	H	R	E	T	I
1	2	3	4	5	6	7	8	9

8 5 7   2 9 1 7 6 3 8 4 6

Write the meaning of the word here. If you don't know, find it in a dictionary.

Fun in the Sun

John F. Kennedy, the thirty-fifth president of the United States, was born in Brookline. His family loved to play football on the lawn of the Kennedy compound on Cape Cod. They also loved to sail. What is wrong in this picture?

Very Short Biographies

Here are eight people from Massachusetts who did something important.
Can you match each sentence to its drawing?

Leonard Bernstein, a famous composer, was born in Lawrence.

Percival Lowell, an astronomer, helped discover the planet Pluto.

Johnny Appleseed, a pioneer whose real name was John Chapman, was born in Leominster.

William Monroe, from Concord, manufactured the first pencils.

Vannevar Bush, from Everett, helped develop the modern computer.

Eli Whitney, born in Westborough, invented the cotton gin.

Elias Howe, born in Spencer, invented the sewing machine.

Luther Burbank, a native of Lancaster, bred the Idaho potato.

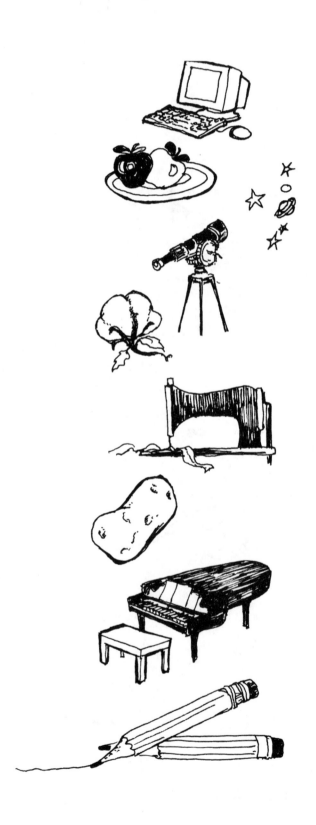

ANSWER KEY

Page 3:

Page 4:

Page 7:

Page 8:

Page 9:

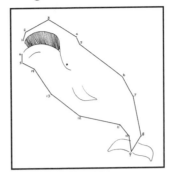

Page 10:

Page 11:

Page 12:
CAN'T CATCH ME

Page 13:

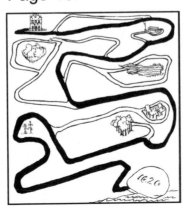

Page 14:
MAYFLOWER

Page 15:
PILGRIMS
LONG
YOUNG
MANY
ONLY
USED
THEY
HARVEST

Page 16:

S	A	M	U	E	L	E	I	S
J	U	D	Y	R	X	L	I	U
J	O	H	N	N	V	I	Z	Z
K	F	I	J	I	Q	Z	N	I
S	T	R	O	E	Z	A	O	E
I	R	A	S	Z	O	B	N	T
R	E	M	E	M	B	E	R	H
I	S	C	P	A	T	T	W	A
C	O	T	H	A	R	Y	D	N
H	L	O	N	R	W	H	B	K
A	V	E	O	Y	D	O	I	F
R	E	R	N	B	S	L	S	U
D	D	Q	M	L	O	V	E	L
W	R	E	S	T	L	I	N	G

Page 17:
DEER, TURKEY

Page 18:

C	O	O	K	I	E	S	O	P	M	Z
A	C	H	I	C	K	E	N	U	I	Q
F	I	S	H	L	G	M	T	M	K	E
I	T	Q	U	A	I	C	J	P	K	G
G	U	U	T	I	D	O	L	K	N	G
C	R	A	N	B	E	R	R	I	E	S
D	K	S	L	U	E	N	H	N	U	T
R	E	H	N	G	R	A	P	E	S	A
I	Y	A	M	S	S	O	D	A	Z	E

Page 19:
HAPPY HOLIDAYS

Page 21:

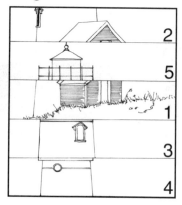

Page 22:

Page 23:

L	E	S	C	A	L	L	O	P		
L	J	I	H	E	L	A	D	O		
O	A	F	E	H	A	C	L	A	M	
B	M	L	R	A	B	E	E	F		
S	W	O	R	D	F	I	S	H		
T	H	U	I	D	I	C	O	D		
E	E	N	N	O	A	T	S	T	U	
R	A	D	G	C	R	A	B	N	A	
W	T	E	X	K	A	L	F			
S	H	R	I	M	P	Z	E			

Page 24:

60

Page 25:
FARMER

Page 26:

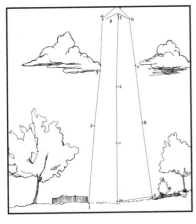

Page 28:
DAMPN; DAN, PAN,
NAP, MAP, MAN, DAMP,
PAD, and others

Page 29:

SILVER

IRON

COPPER

Page 30:
MOTHER GOOSE

Page 31:
NEW YORK
VERMONT
NEW HAMPSHIRE

Page 32:

M	E	R	R	I	M	A	C	K	S	O
X	H	O	U	S	A	T	O	N	I	C
R	H	I	N	D	A	N	U	B	E	L
U	V	O	L	E	L	B	E	H	R	O
C	O	N	N	E	C	T	I	C	U	T
H	L	I	B	R	X	Z	Q	O	D	A
A	G	L	A	F	T	O	N	N	I	I
R	A	E	T	I	V	E	X	C	W	T
L	O	E	S	E	I	N	E	O	F	Y
E	A	S	T	L	U	D	Q	R	G	I
S	S	H	U	D	S	O	N	D	L	A

Page 33:

Page 34:

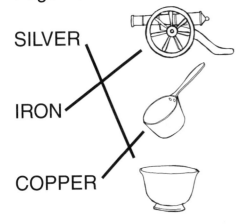

61

Page 35:
WEBSTER

Page 36:

Page 37:
BOSTON

Page 38:

Page 39:

Page 40:

TED WILLIAMS

Page 41:

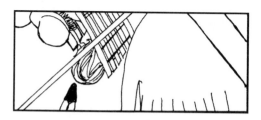

Page 42:
CAT IN THE HAT
MAKE WAY FOR DUCKLINGS
GREEN EGGS AND HAM
GOODNIGHT MOON
MOTHER GOOSE TALES
HOP ON POP
MIKE MULLIGAN AND HIS STEAM
SHOVEL

Page 43:
I PLEDGE ALLEGIANCE TO THE FLAG
OF THE UNITED STATES OF AMERICA,
AND TO THE REPUBLIC FOR WHICH IT
STANDS, ONE NATION UNDER
GOD, INDIVISIBLE, WITH LIBERTY AND
JUSTICE FOR ALL.

Page 44:

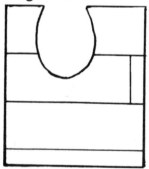

Page 45:

Page 46:

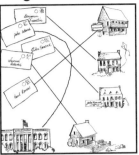

Page 47:
DENTIST

Page 48:

Page 49:

Page 50:
FRANCIS, FREELAN

Page 51:

Page 53:
READING IS FUN

Page 54:

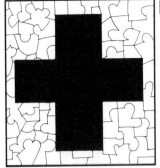 RED CROSS

Page 55:

Page 56:
THE LIBERATOR; one who sets free

Page 57:

Page 58:

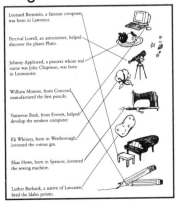

Take Off with the *Alpha Flight Books* Series!

Here's a series of hardcover jacketed ABC books that teach children the alphabet while also giving them interesting information about each letter's topic. The series is designed for the preschool and beginning reader, but its format and fun facts make it suitable for ages 4-8. Each letter of the alphabet has a two-page spread consisting of:
• the letter in both upper and lower case   • a three- to four-sentence explanation of each letter's topic
• a photograph   • illustrations

"C" is for California
1892920271 • $17.95

"C" is for Canada
1892920301 • $17.95

"M" is for Missouri
1892920263 • $17.95

"M" is for Missouri's Rocks and Minerals
1892920298 • $17.95

"T" is for Texas
189292028X • $17.95

"F" is for Firefighting
1892920204 • $17.95

"I" is for Illinois
1892920417 • $17.95

"M" is for Massachusetts
1892920425 • $17.95

"M" is for Michigan
1892920433 • $17.95

"N" is for New York
1892920441 • $17.95

GHB Publishers

3906 Old Highway 94 South, Suite 300 / St. Charles, Missouri 63304
888-883-4427 / FAX: 636-441-7941 / www.ghbpublishers.com